READ FOR FUN

your Children Use BOOK

PATRICK'S WORKSHOP

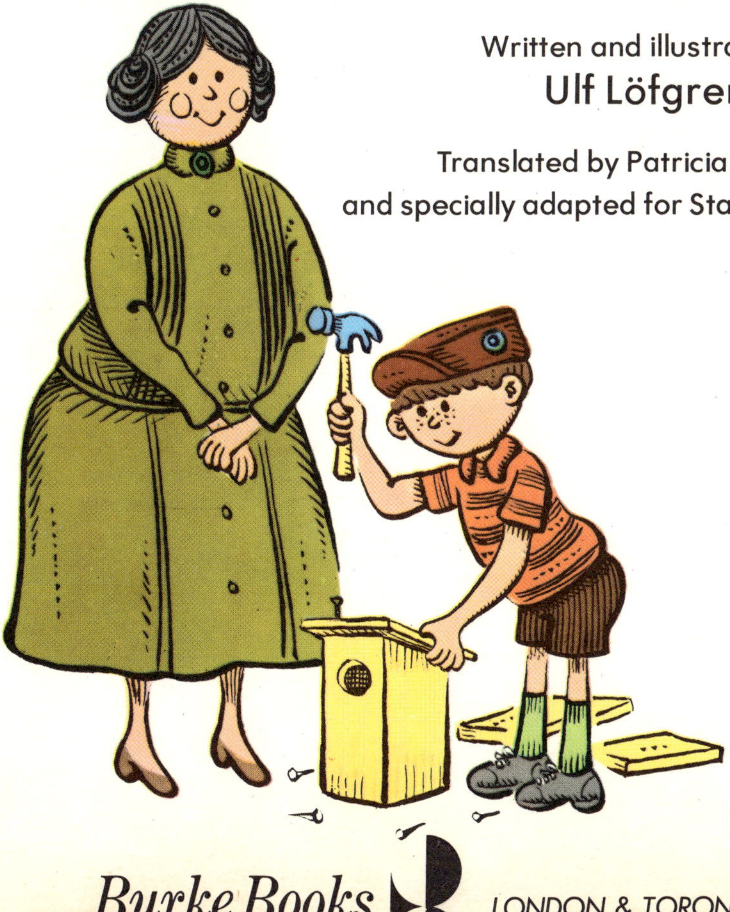

Written and illustrated by
Ulf Löfgren

Translated by Patricia Crampton
and specially adapted for Stage Three readers

Burke Books LONDON & TORONTO

Patrick was a clever boy who had very good ideas and could make all kinds of things. There was nothing he liked better than woodwork and hammering and painting.

Patrick spent nearly all his time doing woodwork. But his mother did not like him doing carpentry in the kitchen. The noise made her head hurt, she said.

One day when Patrick's granny came to see them his mother said, "I don't think I can bear all this hammering in the kitchen much longer."

Patrick's granny nodded. She knew it was difficult, having to listen to all that banging all day long.

"Do you know," said Granny after a time, "when I come to think of it, I have a room in my house where I could let Patrick work. It is quite empty and no use at all."

"Do you really mean it?" said Patrick's mother. "Won't that be lovely, Patrick? You can have a room of your own to work in."

"You can use the room beside the garage, which has its own door out into the garden. It will be like a real workshop," said Granny.

"I know," said Patrick. "I shall start a workshop and it will be called PATRICK'S HIGH-SPEED WORKSHOP, because I do everything so quickly."

Next day Patrick moved all his things round to Granny's. The room was quite full of carpenter's tools and pieces of wood and tins of paint.

"I think you had better have a nice workman's cap," said Granny.

She brought out a very special cap which she had found in the garage.

"That's good!" said Patrick.

"Look what I found in the shed," said Granny.

"That's good!" said Patrick. "But what if I have so much work that I can't answer the telephone?"

"I can look after the telephone for you and take all the orders," said Granny.

"That's good," said Patrick.

Patrick turned the old box car into a van.
Now he had a really good workshop van.

Granny helped him to paint signs for the high-speed workshop.

"What kind of workshop were you thinking of having?" asked Granny.

"It's going to be a workshop for everything," said Patrick.

"Everything?" said Granny.

"That's right," said Patrick.

"Do you think it looks nice?" asked Granny.

"Yes, it looks good," said Patrick.

On the very first day Mrs. Green walked by and saw the signs outside Patrick's high-speed workshop.

"Have you really started a workshop for everything, Patrick?" she asked.

"Yes, that's right," said Patrick.

"Then perhaps you can help me. My sink is stopped up and I have a dripping tap, too," said Mrs. Green.

"We'll soon put that right," said Patrick.

"What is wrong with it?" asked Mrs. Green.

"Something stuck in the pipe," said Patrick. "But it's all right now. I have changed the taps, too, and the new ones won't drip any more."

"What luck that I found you to help," said Mrs. Green.

When Patrick got back, Granny was sitting at the office table.

"An order has come in for ten bird boxes, twenty bread boards and a rowing-boat," she said.

"With oars?" asked Patrick.

"Yes," said Granny.

"Ten bird boxes...

and twenty bread boards...

...and a rowing-boat with oars.

That's done," said Patrick.

"Mr. Peters telephoned," called Granny, when Patrick came into the office.

"He has bought an old house which he wants to have painted."

Patrick drove round to Mr. Peters at once.
"The house looks really dirty," said Mr. Peters.

"First I must wash the walls, then mend the holes, and last comes the painting," said Patrick.

"Will it take long?" said Mr. Peters.

"Two days," said Patrick. "Mine is a high-speed workshop."

"I want it painted in bright colours," said Mr. Peters.

"That will be all right," said Patrick.

17

"I am very pleased," said Mr. Peters when Patrick had finished painting.

Just as Patrick got back to his workshop the telephone rang and Granny answered it. "He will come at once," she said and put down the telephone.

"The train has stopped and no one can get it going. Please go at once," said Granny.

Patrick drove off at top speed.

When he got to the train the people were getting very cross. They were shouting at the two engine-drivers, who could not make the engine go.

"What's wrong, then?" asked Patrick.

"The engine! It won't work," said one engine-driver.

"Mostly it says *bompettibompettibom*, but today it said *bimpellibimpellibim* and then stopped," said the other.

"We'll soon put that right," said Patrick, and he climbed into the engine. He turned something here and put a little oil there from his oil can.

"Now you can start the engine," he said.

Patrick was right. They all thanked him as the train moved off saying *bompettibompettibom*.

"My dear boy, you must be quite tired out after all that work," said Granny when Patrick came back. "Now I think you must have a little holiday."

"That's good!" said Patrick. "There's nothing I like better."

TRANSLATED AND ADAPTED FROM "PATRIKS SNABBVERKSTAD" © ULF LÖFGREN 1969
THIS TRANSLATION FIRST PUBLISHED AUGUST 1975
© BURKE PUBLISHING COMPANY LIMITED 1975
ILLUSTRATIONS © ULF LÖFGREN 1969

All rights reserved. No part of this publication may be reproduced, stored in a retrieval system, or transmitted, in any form or by any means, electronic, mechanical, photocopying, recording or otherwise, without the prior permission of Burke Publishing Company Limited or Burke Publishing (Canada) Limited.

ISBN 0 222 00076 7 HARDBOUND
ISBN 0 222 00082 1 LIMP
ISBN 0 222 00053 8 LIBRARY

BURKE PUBLISHING COMPANY LIMITED, 14 JOHN STREET, LONDON WC1N 2EJ.
BURKE PUBLISHING (CANADA) LIMITED, P.O. BOX 48, TORONTO-DOMINION CENTRE, TORONTO 111, ONTARIO.
PRINTED IN GREAT BRITAIN BY
WILLIAM CLOWES & SONS, LIMITED. LONDON, BECCLES AND COLCHESTER